NINJA
SECRETS OF
INVISIBILITY

NINJA
SECRETS OF
INVISIBILITY

ASHIDA KIM

CITADEL PRESS   SECAUCUS, N.J.

CONTENTS

FOREWORD

"Looked for, they cannot be seen; listened for, they cannot be heard; felt for, they cannot be touched."
—**Old Ninja Legend**

The training a student must undergo in order to become a practicing Ninja involves tasks that are not to be taken lightly; indeed, attaining the higher stages demands an intensity of effort and perseverance greater than that required for any other pursuit. For this is the Great Work *(Ta Tso)*. The training process necessitates the disintegration and reintegration of the student's own personality. As a result, one may become a Man of Knowledge.

In attempting such alterations, one would be well advised to proceed cautiously. It may be that some particular personality trait is the keystone which supports much of the personal self. To eliminate or amplify such a trait or flaw, even to replace it with an unprepared role model, can be dangerous. In fact, it can be fatal. It may be helpful to keep in mind the following saying: "Through wisdom is the Ninja created, through understanding is he established, through mystery is he maintained." The best guidance in such endeavor is one's *sensei;* barring this, daily practice is recommended.

There is a peculiar interaction between the personalities of the sensei and the apprentice, and it is in this atmosphere that the best lessons are taught. Such lessons cannot be learned from a book. However, with the aid of this book, it may be possible to reach a level within oneself where such a personal link can be achieved. Then, by eternal law, the Master will appear when the student is ready. Long before this occurs, the student will have met that teacher through the personalities which have guided him along the path. Whenever he is ready for the next stage of his training, the appropriate instructor for that stage will come to him. The true Masters and Initiates of the Art do exist, but they do not advertise.

In the end, one must remember that there is only one true Master, the inner self, who dwells behind the mask of the apprentice. This inner, higher self is merely a facet of the eternal, one with the ten thousand things, the ultimate court of appeal, the True Master, and indeed the true Ninja.

PREFACE

In Ninjitsu, it is often taught that all things are found in the Great Game. In order to maintain a modicum of security and to make the game more interesting, the Ninja surrounds himself with an air of mystery. This "attitude" is much the same as the magician's "magical personality." The Ninja never reveals anything about himself and only occasionally confirms any information which might be presented as knowledge about him. Since the times when Ninjitsu was outlawed in Japan, and even prior to that time in the ranks of the Chinese espionage services, no true agent would admit his affiliation with any clan, since to do so meant almost certain death by torture. Many rumors and myths surround the Silent Way—that is why it is silent.

There is a saying in stage magic that "the more a story is told, the larger it becomes." And who is to say that the "tall tales" concerning one's exploits do not have *some* basis in fact? Certainly the Ninja were the finest warriors of their day, and the daring adventures of many a bold man have spun the stuff of legends.

Therefore, be mysterious. It adds spice to the game, an edge to the spirit, and armor for the body. Keep your own council. Never eat or drink in public. Make no show of strength or ability, but be humble in all things.

To the Ninja, especially the Yamabushi, the outside world was a hostile world, with enemies everywhere. They were particularly skillful at adapting the ancient Tantric lore that had made its way to Japan. It is from the Yamabushi that most of the known history of Ninjitsu exists. Because of the security precautions needed in those bygone days, the information we do have today is fragmentary at best. One thing is clear, however: all of the clans maintained an air of terror within their domains.

One may question why presumably peaceful, ascetic priests would develop reputations as the deadliest assassins in history, with a feudal clan network more than capable of dreadful retribution. Perhaps this was one way of keeping the curious away, and it certainly didn't hurt when fees were to be negotiated. Machiavelli had said that "it is better to be feared than loved; for when the people fear you, they will do all in their power to gain your favor and seek your advice; but when they love you and sing the praises of your benevolence, they will use you and manipulate you for their own ends." Even before Machiavelli made his observations on power, the same philosophy was known to the Ninja.

One must master the art of war in order to instill the type of fear referred to by Machiavelli. In order to do so, one must acquire the understanding of strategy, whose primary element is to confuse the enemy. The tricks given here are the most difficult in the Silent Way and are primarily related to stealth. A thorough knowledge of stealth will enable you to penetrate anywhere, unseen.

1. SECRETS OF INVISIBILITY

Invisibility, like beauty, is in the eye of the beholder. Therefore, since there are no magic rings or potions which can render us unseeable, the Ninja appropriately chose to direct their attention to the eye of the beholder. In this regard, they developed the art of *HsiMenJitsu (Saiminjitsu* in Japanese) or "Way of the Mind Gate." Quite possibly, this work represents the earliest study of human psychology yet uncovered.

Concurrently, there evolved the Kuji-Kiri form of meditation. By experiencing his emotions, the student was taught to also experience the depths of psychological morbidity, thereby learning not only to master them within himself, but also to manipulate them in others to achieve his own ends. As in the evolution of most Ninjitsu methods, there are initially three basic tenets: Power, Love, and Wisdom (Yin, Yang, Tao; Positive, Negative, Neutral; etc.)

Power is defined here as performing an act because it is one's will to do so. This presupposes that one is capable of rational decisions. Love is the reverse of rational decision, for you are thus doing the will of someone else. Wisdom is knowing the difference. These are the goals of all mankind. Simply stated, they are the stakes in the Great Game.

The principles of the Five Feelings and Desires, all of which interact according to the Law of the Five Elements, are studied. In the techniques of stealth, this study is known as *Nyudaki no Jitsu,* which means to overcome the enemy or a guard by discovering his weaknesses.

1

The first of the Five Feelings is *Kosha,* the desire for sensual satisfaction. An enemy susceptible to this attack might be bribed, lured into a compromising situation, or be flattered into revealing information. In later times, drug dependence or offers of forbidden items were used as incentives. Vanity and the overindulgence of appetites are the hallmarks of this type of feeling.

The desire to be of service and the desire for concurrent reward in emotional terms was the second strongest of the Five Desires. Where the first might be considered a desire for power, this second principle, called *Aisha,* represents the psychological need for love. The manipulation of a sympathetic heart is often regarded as somewhat cruel, but then, spies have always had a reputation for ruthlessness.

Kyosha (the power of fear) was used at times to intimidate the enemy when he demonstrated a lack of ego strength. Direct commands, as well as browbeating and the frequently employed "guilt trip," work well on those individuals who succumb to Kyosha.

When an enemy showed a lackadaisical attitude toward his activities or was frequently caught napping by his superiors, a skillful Ninja would offer rank or special privileges to the offender. Promises of less work and more respect often induced a "lazy" enemy to operate in the interest of the Ninja. This process was known as *Rakusha.*

The last, and possibly the most dangerous, of the Five Feelings was the principle of *Dosha* (anger). Inducing the enemy to do something rash or untimely is usually easy. Gauging the degree of his response, however, is sometimes difficult. An enemy who acts quickly often does so with all his might, and a man with a short temper is always to be reckoned with. Still, if one can evade the attack or be prepared with a suitable trap, the adversary will normally expend himself in the first onslaught and find himself cut off from support. Psychologically, he is thus the most vulnerable.

Diagnosing which of these traits the enemy is most likely to fall for is a fine art among the Ninja. Magicians have a term known as "cold reading," a term for the mind-reading effects that rely on basic characteristics common to most subjects. This is modified by the individual's psychological assessment of the enemy. Some information may be deduced from the adversary's body language, while some of it may be discovered by carefully fishing for information. A common example of the latter process may be seen in almost any newspaper today. Many newspapers carry a daily horoscope column. The "predictions" are based on long-known biorhythmic cycles and certain generalizations which may apply to anyone, given the right circumstances. Memorize a few of these predictions and recite them earnestly to someone. The effect of relating this "secret knowledge" about a person is frequently profound.

The Ninja, never being ones to make any test or training regimen too easy, almost always directed their techniques of invisibility against the most difficult opponent they could find. Many of the techniques which are given here, therefore, refer to the guard or sentry. An alert and well-motivated Samurai, schooled in the martial arts and dedicated to his duty, was considered to be the most difficult opponent to overcome. For this reason they were the "test."

Attacking a sentry successfully depends entirely on preparation, assuming, of course, a certain degree of proficiency in the movements of the attack is mastered. The Ninja who selects to attack a sentry should be an expert at stalking, and the attack should be made during the hours of twilight or dark of night. Secondly, the sentry should be observed long enough for the Ninja to become familiar with his characteristic gestures and movements. Lastly, the Ninja should not be encumbered by any unnecessary equipment; all loose portions of his uniform should be "bloused" to prevent snagging

or rustling, and the weapon, if one is used, should be camou-
flaged.

The successful execution of any "pass" on a sentry using
the Art of Invisibility is largely based on what is known in
fencing as the "Tactics of Mistake." The tactic is to launch a
series of attacks, each of which invites a riposte, so that a
pattern of interplay exists between the combatants. The purpose of the aggressor, however, is not to strike home with
any of these preliminary attacks, but rather to carry the
opponent's sword a bit more out of line with each engagement without the opponent taking notice. In the final
engagement, when the blade has been drawn entirely out of
line, the aggressor thrusts home, scoring against an essentially unprotected defender.

In short, the purpose of the various techniques of stealth
is to make the enemy doubt his own judgment. Try this experiment: Have your victim play a guessing game with you in
which he guesses which hand holds the coin. Let him win
every time. In short order, he will increasingly hesitate before
making his selection, afraid not of finding the coin, but
rather of ending his lucky streak.

The techniques of vanishing are similar to the coin game
in that most involve a magical technique known as an acquitment. A magician's hand which is shown to be empty when
it actually contains a vanished object is a good example of
an acquitment. Acquitments are seldom convincing in stage
magic and in the *Sun Shih K'an Chien Chih*. Most take advantage of the confusion of the moment to be truly effective.

2. TERMINOLOGY

Certain terms will be employed in this book to describe the type of action required for certain movements, many of which have an archaic derivation. In an effort to make the meaning of these esoteric terms more clear, the following definitions are provided.

Jung Hua (melt). This is the action of sinking into a tub of very hot water. The progress is slow but inevitable as the water envelops the body completely. It is a silent movement, often from one shadow to another.

Ya (press). An ancient Ninja meditative technique in which the student "becomes one" with an object. It is a static act, normally performed upon exhalation.

Hua Ch'u (slip). A quick movement, usually employing a side-step action, which is executed with the back facing a barrier.

Ti Lao (drop). A term meaning to fall flat onto the chest, executing the front breakfall. This is the quickest method of avoiding almost any attack, since the body is removed almost instantly from the field of fire. When properly performed, this movement is silent.

T'iao Ch'i (spring). A quick uncoiling movement. It is indeed a very fast movement.

Yin Ni (concealment). To be hidden from the view of the enemy but not necessarily his fire.

Chi Kai (cover). A position of concealment which also shields

5

one from the field of fire or line of engagement.

Ch'ieh Shih (peep). Pertains to observing the enemy while remaining unseen. The action is one of looking quickly from a position of concealment; i.e., to view the enemy by means of a peephole or a quick look around the corner.

Ch'ien Hsing K'an (peek). The action of observing the enemy from concealment by slowly bringing the eyes into play, exposing as little of the body as possible, and quickly withdrawing out of sight when the evaluation is complete.

P'ieh Chien (glance). To observe the enemy by quickly looking in his direction.

I P'ieh (glimpse). To observe the enemy for only an instant in passing. This action requires the ability to evaluate quickly and at a later time than when the observation is made.

Pien Pieh (sideways glance). To observe the enemy, moving the eyes only, when he is looking in the other direction. (Note: When the enemy looks toward the observer, that observer must look away without moving.) This technique may be used in public.

Chu Shih (stare). To observe the enemy, using peripheral vision, without moving the eyes.

Ch'ien Shih (watch). To observe the enemy for a specific period of time.

Kuan Ch'a (observe). To look at the enemy and evaluate his situation as completely as possible.

Hsing Tsia. Refers to a go-behind step. Chapter 6, Escapes and Reversals, contains many movements which utilize this type of step.

One thing should be said concerning the various methods of observing the enemy: the methods all require that no eye contact be made with the adversary. It is an unusual quirk of humans that they are able to "sense" eye contact. Try this experiment: select two volunteers and have them stand apart, facing a wall, at least twenty feet ahead of you. Direct them to face the wall and to turn around and look at you if they "feel" you are looking at them. If they do not sense that you are specifically looking at one of them, they should continue facing the wall.

Perform this experiment, looking at one of the volunteers. Concentrate on calling the volunteer "mentally" if you wish, but focus your attention on the nape of the neck of whichever person you want to have turn to you. Amazingly enough, the correct volunteer will turn about 75 percent of the time. Random chance dictates that half of the time the correct volunteer will turn around; therefore, the test cannot be repeated too many times. If one volunteer is selected more often than the other, the second volunteer will frequently turn, "hoping" you are looking at him in an effort to join in the game.

Most volunteers who have tried this test report a prickly feeling or a feeling of warmth on the back of the neck, which prompts them to turn. Whether this is what is known as telepathy or intuition is unknown and meaningless. It is the proof of the theory which is of significance.

3. GAME OF
THE STONES

In order to train the Ninja in the proper method of observing the enemy so that he may obtain as much useful and specific information as possible, the masters have devised the following method:

Obtain a small wooden box with a lid, a jewelry box, or a shallow bamboo/wicker dish with a cover. Place small stones, jewelry, bits of glass, keys, buttons, checkers, coins, or any similar items into the selected container until the bottom is covered one layer deep. There should be several sets of two, three, and so on, of each item. Do not initially include items which contain too much detail, but you may do so later as the game becomes more complicated due to the increased skill of the student. It is best for the sensei or some other party to select the items and the container for the student, since the student would otherwise easily remember the items if he were to pick them himself for the test.

Place the container in front of the student with the lid or cover closed. Open or uncover the container, exposing the contents to view. Instruct the student to look at the items, study them for as long as desired—even touching and examining them for as long as desired.

When the student has examined the items, cover the contents once again and ask the student to name the objects and their number. Check his accuracy. At first, his recollection will be minimal. So that the student does not become disappointed at his inability to remember every item and its number perfectly, the container should not initially contain too many items.

When this exercise has been completed, uncover the container once more and allow the student to check his own accuracy. Help him with the counting by first selecting one item. For instance, have him note that there are five turquoise stones, three emeralds, etc., and note whether the student actually counts the turquoise stones or takes your word for it. Repeat the entire exercise, covering the container and asking the student to name, number, and identify the contents. Wait until the student is finished; the test should be simple so that the student will now be able to more accurately remember the type and number of contents.

Check his accuracy, noting especially whether he correctly states that there are six (rather than five) turquoise stones. If he says there are five, as you told him, you may now teach him that he should *never* accept hearsay information and should *always* confirm such information from his own experience.

If the student is correct in saying there are actually six turquoise stones and is accurate in the other counts and characteristics of this exercise, remove the container and contents from view and *tell* him the trick of the five/six stones so that he is aware of it. Reinforce his skill in observation with a compliment, observing his reaction.

Ask the student to describe the container which held the Game of the Stones. Check his accuracy. He will almost certainly make some error in his description, most probably making many inaccurate statements. This is because once the game is begun, he will concentrate on the contents and not on the container. At this time you may teach him the second lesson of the game: don't miss the forest for the trees. Do not become so absorbed in detail that the overall picture is obscured.

Repeat the game at another time with different contents. The container may remain the same since once the student is aware of the trick (observing the container as well as its contents), he will not be fooled by it again. Avoid the first "trick" (telling him the incorrect number of certain items), until the level of difficulty becomes so great that the student is unable to accurately supply the required information after three successive attempts.

You may now teach him the third lesson of the game: the memory peg system. This is a magical/mentalist system for remembering a large number of differing items for a short period of time. Many good peg systems exist, and much has been written on them in numerous books on magic. The student should research this and determine which system is best for him. For example, select a word which rhymes with each sequential number: one would be "sun," two would be "blue," three would be "tree," etc. Each item that is named is assigned a sequential peg. For example, if the first item is a watch, the student would visualize a watch in the sun; the second item being a radio would cause a visualization of a blue radio; and the third object would call up the image of a book in a tree. Proceed in a similar manner as far as needed. Any number which is called for will immediately trigger the peg with which it rhymes and the visualized picture will identify the required item. "Three" would remind the student of a book in a tree, and he would consequently respond by saying "book."

This system is easily mastered from one to ten, while going up to fifty requires only a little practice. Some mentalists can peg to one hundred (although this many items are seldom used since one hundred spectators calling out items would take all night). To peg eleven to nineteen, use the one peg (sun) and the appropriate integral digit for each visualization. For example, if the watch was named eleventh, the student would visualize a watch under *two* suns; likewise, if the radio were named twelfth, a blue radio in the sun would be visualized. All of the "twenties" would be blue, all of the "thirties" would be in the trees, etc.

Items memorized in this manner will be actively retained by the memory for about three days. With repetition, the period of recall may be extended indefinitely. This is possible because the memory more easily recalls those items which are odd or unusual, and the pegs make every item unusual. The retention quickly fades because odd items are normally somewhat rare, though they may attract and arrest the attention for a short time. Not being a part of everyday existence, they are more easily forgotten, and the pegs are usually reused for new items in short order. Therefore, the student need have no fear that he will awaken abruptly from a sound sleep and begin reciting items.

This form of training may be further complicated by allowing the student to look at the contents of the container for shorter and shorter lengths of time until he can accurately name the contents with little more than a glance. By this stage, the student will be beyond the peg system and will instead be visualizing the entire contents of the container and reciting and counting them from memory. He is now "classroom trained" to observe properly. He must now acquire practical field experience.

4. ART OF STEALTH

The lost track form, also known as the *Mi Lu Kata,* has been transmitted to the Ninja from Tibet. It is composed of eighty-one movements, some of which are detailed here, while others are contained in other segments of this book. Since it was always preferred that the Ninja work alone, training in the Art of Invisibility was made available to every *Genin,* a Ninja of the lowest rank, in the *Koga Hai-Lung Ryu.* Skill in disguising one's numbers on a mission was essential to the individual's survival. This was generally done in one of two ways: making it appear that more than one Ninja was on the premises, or making it appear that no Ninja were about—hence the requirement of invisibility.

Together with *Inpo* (hiding) techniques, techniques for penetrating the enemy camp by passing armed and unarmed guards may be considered the means by which one remains invisible. They compose the subsection of Ninja training known as the Art of Stealth *(Pi Mi Hsing Tung).*

Techniques designed to escape the enemy should he discover your position will also be discussed. These are known as Vanishing Methods *(Sun Shih K'an Chien Chih).* They may be used to create confusion in the mind of the enemy.

Should the unthinkable occur—you are not only discovered, but also seized—this book's final section will enable you to reverse the enemy's hold and gain a position behind him. It will soon be apparent that such information is the single most important factor in these movements.

PENETRATING UNSEEN

Once the art of hiding (Inpo) is mastered, one can remain unseen virtually at will. The ability to penetrate the enemy's camp unseen *(T'ou Ju Pu K'o Chien Te),* however, requires that one be capable of quick movement. To accomplish this, study the field of view of the human eye. Take into consideration all the factors which may restrict that field, including the limits of peripheral vision. Learning to do so will enable you to stay "out of sight, out of mind."

The limits of one's peripheral vision may be determined in the following manner: stand erect with the feet together, arms extended to the sides, forming a "T." Point the index finger toward the ceiling, look straight ahead, and slowly bring the fingertips into view simultaneously on the left and right. The point at which you first catch sight of the finger on each side is the limit of your peripheral vision on that side. This limit will vary with individuals but, generally speaking, you should be able to see both fingers when your arms are directly out to both sides. Some degree of vision defect may be indicated if it is necessary for you to bring your fingers closer toward the center.

The accompanying diagram and photographs illustrate the limits of peripheral vision. Looking at the diagram, you can see the sentry standing at Parade Rest with his eyes aimed straight ahead. The wall behind him represents the limits of his peripheral vision if he were well trained in observation. The key here is that his attention remain fixed straight ahead. The first angle of the wall represents the degree of vision afforded the sentry when he moves his eyes left or right without turning his head.

The shaded areas around the sentry show the limits of his peripheral vision around the area of his feet. The lighter area

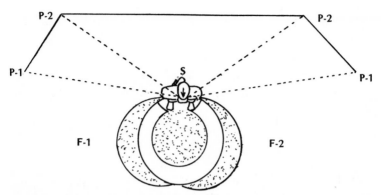

Diagram A: Field of Vision as Seen from Above

S to P-1 represents the limits of peripheral vision, side to side, in the "eyes front" position. S to P-2 represents the limits of peripheral vision, side to side, when the eyes are turned left or right and the head is kept still.

F-1, the light, O-shaped area, is the boundary of the field of view of the ground around the feet when the eyes face straight ahead. The shaded areas, F-2, are the boundaries of the field of view on the ground around the feet when the eyes move but the head does not.

It is interesting to note that it is impossible to see one's own feet if one's eyes look straight ahead.

is the "eyes front" range, while the darker area indicates his range when he looks down without moving the head.

It should be remembered that all movements executed behind the sentry must be silent, since any noise may attract his attention. An excellent time to utilize this technique is during a speech, rally, or a parade.

OUT OF SIGHT, OUT OF MIND

To achieve this goal of out of sight, out of mind *(Wai Te Shih Li/Wai Te Hsin),* first fix your attention on a spot at the base of the enemy's skull. In this way, you will be able to detect and predict the movements of his head and eyes. In order to be successful at predicting these movements, it is necessary that you practice predicting such movements every day. Most movements are made in a leisurely manner, so a quick Ninja, using one of his many silent steps, should be able to stay out of sight. Once the field of view has been established, keep low in your stance, remembering that your adversary's shoulders block his side vision to some degree. Be sure to move slowly when in the area illustrated in the previous diagram, since a quick movement is likely to be seen out of the corner of the eye, thereby revealing your position.

Fig. 1 illustrates the first position of the cross-step *(Heng Pu)*, which will be used to pass behind the sentry. Slightly lower your left shoulder in the direction of the movement. Your knees should be well bent, your back straight, and your body *almost* touching the wall.

By executing the cross-step with the right foot, the Ninja would now be in a closed stance position at the outermost limit of the sentry's field of view. At this point, the eyes are spotted *(Ti Tien)* on the base of the skull. Use the fingers of your left hand to lightly feel your way along the wall. Movement is slow enough so that the feet may be used to feel their way and no noise is made (Fig. 2).

Having gained a relatively secure position behind the sentry out of his field of view, it is now possible to "check the trail" ahead by looking briefly in the direction of the line of march. Once it is determined to be clear of obstruction or bits of rubble which might betray your presence, again fix your attention on the enemy. If possible, try to make this interlude as brief as possible and see that you are in the extended portion of the cross-step, since this provides the best balance and the opportunity to move quickly to either side (Fig. 3).

The next three steps may be taken in rapid succession. The positions in Fig. 4, the cross-step in front, eyes fixed on the enemy, and Fig. 5, the extended cross-step, eyes fixed, fingertips lightly touching the wall, may be assumed. (Bear in mind that *any* contact with a surface such as a wall or fence may produce a scraping sound which will attract attention. Some guidance must still be rendered while the concentra-

FIG. 1

FIG. 2

FIG. 3

FIG. 4

FIG. 5   FIG. 6

tion is riveted on the enemy.) Fig. 6 shows the closed stance
at the limits of the optional field of peripheral vision.

Slowly, move around the outer limit of the enemy's field
of view. Watch his eyes from this vantage point. It will be sur-
prising how much you can tell about where a man is looking
by watching him in this manner. It may be necessary in this
instance to press against the wall in order to muffle any small
sounds made by your tedious passing (Fig. 7).

PENETRATING BY MISDIRECTION

Perhaps the simplest method for passing the enemy without being observed is to direct his attention elsewhere *(Yoji-
gakure no Jitsu). Yoji* is the Japanese term for toothpick.
Since they were often made of ivory (or even metal), they
produced an unusual sound when tossed over the head of a
sentry. Any small pebble, however, will suffice to draw the
sentry's attention, although a piece of glass has been found to

FIG. 7

be most effective since it frequently sounds like the clink of metal and arouses more suspicion. Those Ninja who were skilled in ventriloquism, and there were many, would "throw their voice" to throw the enemy off. They also often imitated the sounds of cats or other small animals to allay the suspicions of some guards.

From a position of concealment, throw a small object over the head of the sentry in such a manner that it is unseen but strikes the ground ahead of him loudly enough to be heard. Maintain a low stance during this movement, as you may be observed from other posts without your knowledge, and keep the movement of your toss slow and graceful, even light. Such a movement is less likely to be seen or heard. Cast the pebble, don't hurl it (Fig. 8).

As the enemy moves forward to investigate, slip around the corner behind him using the entering pivot. Fix your attention on the base of his skull (Fig. 9).

FIG. 8   FIG. 9

As the sentry expands his search by looking to his right, "melt" around the corner and press into the surface in order to eliminate as much of your silhouette as possible. You may remain in this position as long as the sentry merely looks to one side or the other, since you are out of his view (Fig. 10).

When the sentry abandons his search, either because he feels his suspicions were groundless or because he found nothing and decided to return, you make your move. As he turns to his right (most men, especially soldiers, step off with their left foot first, forcing a turn to the right), "fade" into the far corner of the alcove and vanish into the shadows. From here, the enemy may check your original position and find nothing (Fig. 11).

Had the enemy turned to his left in Fig. 11, it would have been necessary for you to retreat back to the first position and try another means by which to pass him. Fig. 12 shows that as long as one remains properly positioned behind the

FIG. 10

FIG. 11

FIG. 12

FIG. 13

FIG. 14

sentry, it is possible to remain outside his field of view while
the second entering pivot is used to pass the alcove (Fig. 12).

It is hoped that the misdirecting noise would be sufficient to draw the enemy far away from his position, but this
is not normally the case. The intruding sound must not be
so great as to cause the sentry to raise an alarm. In any event,
at this juncture, the alcove is passed, and the Ninja peeks
(Shih) around the corner to ensure that the sentry returns
to his former complacent state (Fig. 13).

LOOK BUT DO NOT SEE

Instead of attempting to pass a static enemy position, it
is sometimes more feasible to let the enemy pass *you*. To
accomplish this, it is necessary that your adversary take no
notice of your position *(K'an Ch'u Pu K'an Chien)*. This may
be done by utilizing a familiar object (a tree in the accom-

FIG. 15   FIG. 16

panying photos) that is frequently seen in passing by the guards as they change shifts, or by concealing oneself in a convenient shadow (Figs. 14 and 15). Even though the Ninja may be within the peripheral vision of the sentry in Fig. 16, the sentry overlooks him because the Ninja is not moving and because the object (the tree) has been seen many times by the sentry. There is no motion or silhouette, so in the sentry's mind there is no danger.

As shown in Fig. 14, the Ninja has heard or suspected that the sentry is approaching down the trail. From his position of concealment and cover, the Ninja sees that the guard is unarmed and decides to let him pass.

As the sentry approaches, the Ninja works his way around the tree, remaining out of sight by keeping the obstacle (the tree) *between* himself and the guard (Fig. 15). The Ninja presses against the tree with his back to conceal his silhouette, muffle any noise he may make moving around the

FIG. 17

trunk, and to afford himself a base to push off from should he be forced to run for it.

When the sentry has passed the obstacle, the Ninja moves back in *front* of the tree, becoming "one" with it. Becoming a part of the scenery requires a calm mind above all else (Fig. 16).

As the enemy proceeds down the path to his left, the Ninja moves swiftly and silently down the edge of the path from whence the sentry approached. He does not take the center of the trail, since this would expose his silhouette. He remains low, below the level of the grass or shrubs which mark the path. By using the cross-step (Heng Pu), it is possible to traverse the intervening distance and safely secure the next place of concealment (Fig. 17).

If the sentry should be armed, proceed with the technique of striking from behind *(Ashigaru-Sha),* discussed on page 30.

LOST TRACK PIVOT

The lost track pivot *(Mi Lu Pu)* is the basis for many Ninjitsu movements. Though this step may be used to attack the enemy from behind, let us now turn to how the pattern may be used to create confusion in the mind of the enemy. It is always preferable to pass anyone who is not directly the target of a given penetration. Barring this, it is preferable to leave no armed enemies between yourself and freedom. This demonstration of the Mi Lu Pu step is best used to pass a sentry from behind, since during its execution, the sentry will be manipulated into looking the other way while the Ninja slips by.

Approach the sentry from a position of concealment in a ready stance. Be prepared to spring on him and instantly silence any outcry (Fig. 18).

Stand directly behind the sentry and tap him on the left shoulder (Fig. 19). When he looks slightly over his left shoulder, expecting someone to be standing there, shift to his right side and lower your center (Fig. 20).

The sentry will then look to his right, and seeing no one

FIG. 18   **FIG. 19**

FIG. 20   FIG. 21

to his left, he will turn further to his right. Step to his left side in preparation for his turn (Fig. 21).

As he turns to his right, execute the spinning back pivot and maintain a position behind him (Fig. 22). Note that the Ninja's weight is over his left leg.

In Fig. 23 we see that the unarmed guard did not follow the pattern of the previous example in which the sentry is to continue to turn to the right. In this case, the sentry instead reversed his direction and turned back to the left. The skillful Ninja has merely shifted his weight back over to his right side and dropped out of sight once again.

The enemy, sensing that he has been tricked, turns quickly back to his left by stepping back with his left foot. The Ninja executes the spinning back-pivot in the opposite direction and keeps his attention fixed on the back of the enemy's skull (Fig. 24).

Looking at Figs. 22 to 24, we can see that no matter

FIG. 22   FIG. 23

FIG. 24

FIG. 25

which way the sentry turns, it is possible to remain out of his view by anticipating his movement and being able to swiftly shift weight from one side to the other.

In Fig. 25, the Ninja is prepared to back-pivot to the enemy's right side again should the enemy continue to turn to his left. The Ninja can also strike out instantly with the heel of his right palm if the sentry should "get ahead" and catch sight of him.

The sentry in Fig. 26 has returned to his at-ease stance. The Ninja has moved once again behind him, but in this instance, he maintains a closed stance, ready to move away.

The Ninja moves silently off from the sentry in Fig. 27. He might have taken any direction during the confusion created by the lost track pivot gyrations, but he must always be ready to change direction when the sentry does.

FIG. 26   FIG. 27

PASSING IN THE LOW LINE

We have shown how to direct the enemy's attention to the high line of sight by tapping him on the shoulder. Now we shall direct our attention to passing in the low line *(Je Te Tsu)*. Unless one is looking down, the feet are generally out of view. Having secured a position of concealment below and behind the enemy, survey his position and attitude (Fig. 28).

Approach him closely enough to touch him with your extended hand. Be prepared to spring up and attack the victim should he decide to move before you are ready. In the United States during the thirties a common prank of many school-age children was the "hot foot" in which a lit match was placed in the seam of clothing belonging to an unsuspecting pedestrian. In ancient times, a glowing ember might be placed on a sentry's sandal, or a few hairs might be plucked

out of the foot itself in order to attract attention to the feet
(Fig. 29).

Pinch your victim's ankle. As he senses the pain, he will
assume that he has been bitten by some insect or small ani-
mal. He will seek to determine the nature of this attack,
which, again, is not sufficient to warrant an alarm (Fig. 30).
Roll over to a hands-and-knees position, keeping an obstacle
(a drum in the accompanying photos) between yourself and
the enemy behind which you can conceal yourself.

As your victim searches for an attacker, move off quickly
past his position (Fig. 31). Alternately, you may attack from
the low line by using the double ankle pickup.

DOUBLE ANKLE PICKUP

As the first step in the double ankle pickup technique
(Ashigaru-Sha No. 1), move to a position of concealment be-
hind the sentry (Fig. 32). The key to your success here—as in
Ninjitsu itself—is silence.

The ability to penetrate the camp of the enemy is essential. Therefore, make no sound as you approach it; disturb
as little as possible enroute (in ancient times, the sudden ces-
sation of crickets chirping at night often revealed the presence of an infiltrator). Approach from downwind if feasible
(in Vietnam it was said the enemy could smell the after-
shave and deodorant of the American soldiers). Remember: if
the enemy sees, hears, or even senses your presence, he will
turn around and have you at a decided disadvantage.

From the hands-and-knees position, gather your feet
under your body so that your weight rests on the balls of
both feet. Reach forward and seize your opponent's ankles
from the outside with both hands (Fig. 33). Curl your fingers
in toward the hand and place your thumb against the back of
the victim's calf to facilitate this hold. Obviously, from this
point on, the enemy is aware of your attack. Most likely he
will look down to see what is touching his ankle, especially

FIG. 28

FIG. 29

FIG. 30

FIG. 31

FIG. 32   FIG. 33

since he may be unfamiliar with this sensation. It is essential
that you move quickly to prevent the counterattack and
silence him before he can make an outcry.

Stand up quickly, bending at the waist and stepping
slightly back with the right leg to maintain your balance. Pull
your adversary's legs from under him in an upward and backward direction, in a circular, quarter-arc manner. Your adversary will fall straight downward if this technique is properly
executed. If he does not fall straight downward, he will fall
forward onto his upper body and face (Fig. 34). The impact
of this fall is profound, although a very small amount of
force is actually exerted against the ankles. Normally, the victim's neck is broken.

Nevertheless, make sure of your victim's demise by side-
stepping beside his prone body or stepping between his legs,
and executing a downward side kick to the base of his skull
with the edge of your left or right foot. This action acts to

FIG. 34   FIG. 35

push the skull off the spine and to break the neck. By shifting the weight over the striking leg and driving straight downward, the neck may also be separated at the seventh cervical vertebra (Fig. 35).

Return to your position at your enemy's feet. Seize both ankles as before and drag his body to a place of concealment (Fig. 36).

Leave the area as stealthily as before (Fig. 37).

TRAIL OR WALKING SENTRY

To execute the trail or walking sentry technique (Ashigaru-Sha No. 2), you must first assume a position of concealment alongside the trail or pathway, preferably at a bend or angle, since the enemy will thus have to direct his attention to where he is going. Press against an object (a tree in the accompanying photos) and become one with it. Relax with your weight braced against the trunk, your legs acting

FIG. 36   FIG. 37

as struts for support. In this way, you can remain completely still for long periods. Wait for the approach of the enemy (Fig. 38).

As the enemy passes, preferably turning down the path away from your position, step in quickly behind him and seize his hair from above with your right hand. Jerk his head backward, exposing his throat to attack, and strike down onto his throat with the left *Shuto* (sword hand). Refer to Fig. 39.

This attack should be directed against the trachea (windpipe) and larynx (Adam's apple). The strike should be of sufficient force to ensure that your adversary can make no outcry. Continue to hold his hair. If he is helmeted, reach over his head and seize the forward edge or "bill" to tilt the head back. Strike quickly, as the element of surprise is on your side. You must, however, act swiftly or the enemy will attempt a countermove (Fig. 40).

From the previous position, slide your left arm around your adversary's neck to a point where your left forearm lies in front of his throat. Clench your left fist and grip your left wrist with your right hand. Snatch your left forearm toward you so that the radial side strikes the enemy forcefully in the throat. In the event that the previous blow merely stunned your adversary, this attack will ensure that he cannot call out. Maintain this hold. This position is known as the rear naked strangle *(Hadake-jime).* In its Judo application, the forearm is pulled against the windpipe, acting against the neck to cause unconsciousness by restricting the intake of oxygen. It may take as long as two minutes to render the enemy senseless (Fig. 41).

Retain the stranglehold on the enemy's neck and drop down on your left knee. Hold his head against your shoulder, and squeeze his neck as tightly as possible as you bear him down to the ground. This action is known as a forward

FIG. 38

FIG. 39

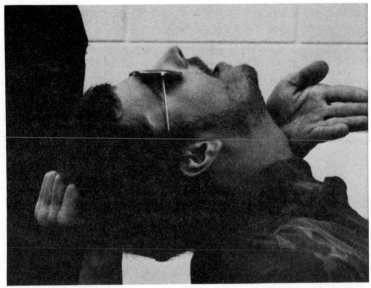

FIG. 40

neck crank, and it will break the enemy's neck. Still keeping the hold, pull your adversary backward to a place of concealment (Fig. 42).

Check the vicinity for any sign that you have been observed, and then move off to your next point of concealment by the shortest route possible (Fig. 43).

LOST TRACK PIVOT

The lost track pivot (Ashigaru-Sha No. 3) is the basis for most of the art of Ninjitsu, and it is therefore imperative that it be mastered. The basis for the invisibility movements is the principle of vision, which states that a finite increment of time exists between the time an individual sees something, identifies it, and then acts upon what he saw. The length of this time lag is very short; therefore, one must move swiftly as well as silently.

FIG. 41

FIG. 43

Move to a position behind the enemy post by using the appropriate Inpo technique (Fig. 44).

As will be seen in the accompanying photographs, it is possible to conceal oneself directly behind the enemy. This may especially be advantageous if one is in danger of being observed by another guard who may be passing by. Tap the enemy lightly on the right shoulder with the fingertips of your right hand. This action is actually a feint, aimed at luring the sentry in the wrong direction at the outset. Psychologically, this will aid in making the enemy doubt his own judgment (Fig. 45).

Anticipating that whoever touched him will be on his right side, the sentry will look to his right. It is at this point that you quickly move down and to the left side of him, remaining outside the range of his peripheral vision. At this moment, you will be totally invisible to the sentry. Direct your attention to the base of his skull, making it possible to anticipate his reactions and guess his next movement (Fig. 46).

Failing to spot anyone on his right side, the guard will naturally suspect that the perpetrator is to his left side. He will then turn sharply toward his left, hoping to catch sight of the perpetrator. Move quickly and silently to the right, closing your stance by drawing your left toes near your right ankle in the hanging foot stance. This position eliminates the possibility that the sentry will glimpse your left foot. Assume a low guard stance defensively with the arms, but do not touch the enemy. Continue to focus your attention on the base of his skull (Fig. 47).

The enemy will continue to turn to his left by stepping to his left rear corner with his left foot. Step forward with your left foot, turning back-to-back with the guard. The first half of the Mi Lu Pu (lost track pivot) has thus been executed. This technique is so named because for a split second the Ninja must turn his back on the enemy temporarily, render-

FIG. 44

FIG. 45

FIG. 46

FIG. 47

FIG. 48   FIG. 49

ing both unseeable. To overcome this, the Ninja employs a technique known in dancing as the point. Knowing that the body must follow the head, the Ninja's attention is focused on the base of the enemy's skull, and he steps as deeply as possible into the technique, whipping the head to look over the left shoulder. The Ninja then steps, shifting the weight over the left leg. It is necessary to pivot on the ball of the right foot and turn as quickly as possible (Fig. 48).

The guard has almost completed his turn to look behind him. In some cases, after this point, the enemy will again reverse his direction and turn to his right. In this event, you must shift your weight back over the left leg, and reverse your previous step to remain behind the guard. Assuming he continues to turn left, bring your right foot to your left ankle in the hanging foot stance. Step out, pivoting on the ball of your left foot. Step out to your right with your right foot. This completes the second half of the pivot. You have

FIG. 50   FIG. 51

rotated 270 degrees by executing one back-turning pivot and one front-turning pivot. Your adversary has turned only 180 degrees and has taken another step to his rear with his right foot (Fig. 49).

The guard again steps with his left foot, turning to look back in his original direction. Perform the back pivot again, watching his skull, and stay behind him (Fig. 50).

As he finishes a complete rotation, returning to his original position, execute the forward-pivot portion of the lost track step. At this point, you may elect to dart out of sight, thereby passing the sentry without engaging him. You have thus overcome the enemy with no physical contact (Fig. 51).

The sentryhold *(Nyudaki-no-jitsu)* position is seen in Figs. 52 to 54. Nyudaki-no-jitsu, translated from the Japanese, means to "discover a sentry's weaknesses or shortcomings in order to penetrate the enemy camp."

The Ninja steps in quickly behind the guard with his left foot. He simultaneously whips his left forearm around the enemy's neck to strike him in the throat with the first metacarpal joint of the index finger side of his hand. This is known as the ridgehand strike. He then punches his adversary in the kidney with a right uppercut action, thus breaking the enemy's balance to the rear.

The throat strike causes the enemy to draw in his breath sharply, preventing him from making any outcry. The Ninja next employs the Japanese Strangle, or sleeperhold, to finish off his enemy and maintain control of his body.

To do the Japanese Strangle, press the advantage by sliding your left arm further around your victim's neck until his larynx rests in the crook of your elbow. Place your left hand on your right biceps, and put your right hand on the base of the victim's skull. Push his head forward into the notch of your left arm, exerting pressure against both sides of his neck simultaneously. This technique, unlike the rear naked strangle, acts against the carotid artery, shutting off

FIG. 52   **FIG. 53**

the supply of blood to the brain and rendering the enemy unconscious (Fig. 54).

The Japanese Strangle should be effective in five to nine seconds if properly applied. For the coup de grace, extend the fingers of both hands to form "sword hands" (Fig. 55). Place the edge of your left hand directly beneath the base of the enemy's skull, and keep his larynx firmly pressed into the crook of your left arm.

Quickly step back with your right foot, pulling your victim down by the hold. The leverage exerted by this position and the forward snap of the neck will serve to break his neck most efficiently (Fig. 56).

Release the stranglehold (or pull the enemy off by his neck) and seize his shoulders. Roll him to his left, toward the wall. Continue this action until his body lies face against the wall (Fig. 57).

With the body hidden as much as possible without cover, move off and proceed with your mission (Fig. 58).

FIG. 54

FIG. 55

FIG. 56

FIG. 57

FIG. 58

5. VANISHING
AND EVASION
METHODS

Having demonstrated the methods of passing a sentry, which would necessarily include the ability to move silently, we will now move on to the study of vanishing methods *(Sun Shih K'an Chien Chih)* and evasive techniques.

DUCKING OUT OF SIGHT

Doorways offer many opportunities for the skillful Ninja to duck out of sight and vanish. Most of these opportunities depend on the impetus of the enemy's advance to carry him past you while you execute a sudden change of direction to get behind him.

The simplest of these movements is the reverse corner pivot, which consists of two entering pivots in opposite directions. Assume that you are being pursued down a corridor and you see a doorway near you. Unless you have scouted properly, the next room may very well be filled with enemy troops. All you need is an instant to disappear (Fig. 59).

As you near the doorway, extend your right hand and seize the doorjamb, braking and redirecting your momentum (Fig. 60). Strongly pull on the doorframe with your right hand, cross-stepping with your left leg as you swing around the edge of the door (Fig. 61). Throw yourself against the inner wall, stepping out to the right with your right foot.

 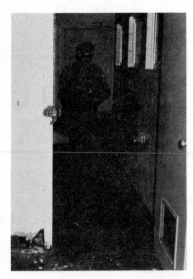

FIG. 59   FIG. 60

Catch the edge of the door with the fingers of your left hand, if necessary, to ensure that you stop inside the edge of the door (Fig. 62).

As your adversary clears the door, cross-step in front with your right leg, gaining a step on the enemy and retaking the doorway. Slip past him quickly by using the second entering pivot. Even if the room were filled with enemy troops, by the time they would see and react to you banging into the wall, the pursuer would be coming into the room. This will momentarily stall any pursuit by them, as your main opponent will block the passageway (Fig. 63).

Pushing off strongly from the doorframe with your left hand, hurl yourself back down the corridor. You will consequently gain a second step on your pursuer. Unless he is skilled in such tactics, the enemy will be unable to stop in time to seize you in passing. The lead gained by this maneuver can easily be used to duck into some nearby hiding spot, thereby vanishing from sight (Fig. 64).

FIG. 61

FIG. 62

FIG. 63

FIG. 64

MELTING STEP

A simple movement upon which many of the vanishing and appearing techniques of Ninjitsu are based is the melting step *(Hsiao Pu)*. Actually, it is not a step at all, but rather a method of dropping out of sight. It is a means by which one may quickly lower one's body to a position at the limits of the enemy's field of vision.

Observe a cat. When it spies its prey, it seems to raise its body slightly and then drop to a crouching position. This is the movement you wish to emulate. To do so, begin by standing in a simple horse stance. Push off with your toes until you're actually on tiptoe. Lower your feet onto the floor, and as your feet contact the ground, let your leg muscles relax as if they were breaking a fall from a great height. In other words, let your body collapse straight down vertically. (Fig. 76 on page 54 illustrates the proper position in which you should end this movement).

Using the melting step, you can execute many types of low motions in order to carry you away from the enemy. It is not always necessary, however, to drop this low. Moreover, the "dip action" of the melting step enables you to remove yourself from the primary areas of attack. Fold yourself into a defensive position, thereby limiting the type of attack the enemy may launch.

Unfortunately this movement is seldom enough to prevent an attack.

SPINNING LEG SWEEP

By far the simplest application of the melting step, commonly seen in many Kung Fu systems, is the spinning leg sweep. It is one of the most devastating takedowns in existence. Easily learned, it is comparatively safe to execute and is effective against your enemy.

In Ninjitsu, the technique is employed as follows: advance half a step on the enemy by assuming a cat stance, keeping your left leg forward and your right leg drawn in. Your one hand should be behind the other, both covering the centerline of your body (Fig. 65).

Lift both hands to attract your adversary's attention and then spread them to the sides, exposing your centerline. Make this motion slowly and deliberately, since the object of this movement is to confuse your enemy into watching your hands by using the limits of his peripheral vision. Strike out at his head in a counterclockwise arc, using a left reverse crescent kick or a snapkick (left front *Ago-geri)* as shown in Fig. 66. Your adversary will then raise his guard and protect his head.

As your left foot touches down from the lead kick, drop down, using the melting step, and allow the momentum of your kick to turn you toward the left rear corner. Pivot on the ball of your right foot and extend the left in a low-sweeping arc. By doing so, you should strike the back of your enemy's knees. Whip your leg around and strike hard (Fig. 67).

FIG. 65

FIG. 66

FIG. 67   FIG. 68

Continue the leg sweep, "reaping" the enemy's legs out from under him and dropping him to the ground (Fig. 68).

FLAT DROP VANISH

The flat drop vanish permits you to vanish when your enemy is very close to you and also enables you to launch a powerful attack to his head. If this technique is utilized at night, the enemy may lose sight of you and break off his attack because he thinks you have vanished.

Assume that your adversary has advanced in an attempt to seize you collar-and-elbow style. You have ducked under his reach and stepped to his outside right line (Fig. 69).

Your enemy would essentially stand in a cross-step in a front stance. He could spin to his left rear and attempt a backfist, but instead he will use the weapon he already has at his disposal: the right crescent kick. This kick arcs up and clockwise, striking at the upper level of the line of attack.

FIG. 69

FIG. 70

The purpose of this kick is for your adversary to fall on you in an "axe kick" type of action. However, instead of trying to stand, you should kick back with both feet and drop, chest first, to the ground. This permits the arc of the reverse crescent kick to pass harmlessly above you. If you are surrounded by darkness, it will seem as if you had vanished, since the enemy's leg crosses his field of view, obscuring your action (Fig. 70).

FIG. 71

FIG. 72

If, however, it is daylight, your enemy may drop his axe kick or change to a heel-stomp in mid-flight. This is unlikely to occur, unless he is highly skilled. Should he resort to a heel stomp (see Fig. 71), quickly execute a right side monkey roll in order to carry you away from the enemy; see Fig. 72. You will wind up in another prone position farther from the enemy. By employing the "push-up appearance" (shown in Figs. 81 and 82), you will confuse your enemy.

VANISHING DRILL

It may be occasionally necessary to remove a sentry without striking him. You will need to make him change his position, without making physical contact, or lead him off on a false track.

The key to the following movement is silent speed. The movement is designed to be performed at night, preferably when the sentry is facing the light source (a campfire, for example). The student, by this time a master of the silent steps, should be sufficiently skilled so as to swiftly execute both forward and reverse shoulder rolls *(Chigari)*.

Having moved to a position behind the guard, snap the fingers of your right hand behind the guard's right ear (Fig. 73) in an attempt to induce him to look over his shoulder. As he begins to turn, shift your weight to your left leg and "drop" both wrists in preparation for hazing *(Kasumi)* the enemy (Fig. 74).

FIG. 73

FIG. 74

FIG. 75   FIG. 76

When your adversary's foot turns to a toed-out position, his head will turn sufficiently for him to see your right hand as it flicks upward under his nose. The sight of your hand will induce him to tilt his head back and close his eyes, or flinch (Fig. 75), which is the objective of hazing.

As your opponent jerks away, immediately drop vertically downward and out of his field of vision. Fix your attention on his forehead, so that you can predict his movements (Fig. 76).

As your enemy recovers, complete the reverse shoulder roll. He will be looking straight ahead, and you should roll out in a flat-prone position, rolling out of his line of vision. Remember that the twist of his body will tend to keep him from turning and possibly glimpsing your position. His eyes, not yet adjusted to the darkness (away from the light source), will be desperately dilating in an attempt to take in more light. As a result, it will be difficult for him to focus his eyes, and he will be uncertain as to what brushed up against his face in the first place (Fig. 77).

At this point, you have "vanished." The first part of this movement achieved practical invisibility and increased the range between you and the sentry by one body length. To ensure that your adversary does not discover your position, execute the monkey roll to your left rear quadrant (Fig. 78) and secure a better position of concealment (Fig. 79). The

FIG. 77

FIG. 78

FIG. 79

two of you are now separated by two body lengths, and you have positioned yourself more directly behind your adversary.

In the Way of the Mind Gate *(Hsi Min Jitsu)*, there exist several techniques for "clouding the mind," of which hazing is one. Just before you made your opponent flinch, he heard a snap, a sound you should now repeat. Psychologically, your opponent will try to be quicker to react this time. From the prone position of concealment, execute a forceful push-up and spring to your feet by gaining enough height from the push so that both feet may be tucked under your center and you land erect without raising or bending your torso (Fig. 80). Simultaneously, snap the fingers of your right hand. The sentry will turn just in time to see you spring from "nowhere," and it does not matter in which direction he turns (Fig. 81).

What the sentry sees as he turns to locate the sound is shown in Fig. 82! Your sudden appearance alone should startle him. The technique of attracting the guard to you so that he may be attacked may also be applied at this time.

FIG. 80

FIG. 81

As the guard turns to attack you, execute a quick side-roll directly toward him. Again, begin this movement by dropping vertically (Fig. 83). Applications of this technique have indicated that one could gain ground so swiftly that a man armed with a firearm could be engaged before he could fire. If your adversary were to fire, the probability is 80 percent that he would overshoot and miss.

At the completion of the side-roll, you are "curled" or "coiled" directly beneath the enemy's center. Even if he were sufficiently confused by the first two appearances, he will al-

FIG. 82

FIG. 83   FIG. 84

most certainly see you roll toward him this time. Remember
that this motion is to be executed preferably in darkness or
in semidarkness. Your enemy should begin to look down as
you finish the roll. The reason he does not strike you immediately is because he is confused. He has not yet been
attacked, only distracted. Moreover, he will anticipate the
third finger snap (Fig. 84).

Allow the momentum of the roll to carry you erect, and
strike out with the right backfist. Hit your enemy on the
right temple before he has a chance to react (Fig. 85). Reload
the right backfist as he falls to the ground (Fig. 86).

It might be said that this is a more elaborate form of the
"passing by misdirection" ploy, and indeed it is. The idea is
first to build on a proven principle and then apply that principle to confuse the enemy. A battlefield analogy might be
to attack the enemy, let him drive off that attack in hot pursuit, and then lure him into an ambush.

EVASIVE DRILL

The following drill is taught in most *ryu* of the *Koga* line
of Ninjitsu. Training in this method is usually begun *before*

any study of the conventional martial arts, which stress the techniques of blocking rather than evading the enemy attack. Since the student will most often employ those techniques which he learns first, he will tend to go to great lengths to avoid confrontation.

Assume a relaxed horse stance (Fig. 87). Face the enemy, who is assuming a modified boxer-frontal stance. Most adversaries who strike first do so with their stronger hand (usually the right one) for their opening blow. They seek to make one powerful, dynamic technique the beginning and the end of the confrontation. Even if such an approach fails, they strike fear into the heart of their opponent. The most common "sucker-punch" is the straight right lead.

Avoid the attack shown in Fig. 88 by shifting to your left side. This movement places the centerline of the body outside the line of attack without tilting the body and significantly altering the level of the hips or shoulders. The shift allows the punch to pass harmlessly over the right shoulder.

FIG. 85

FIG. 86

Once again, do not lean to the left. Push off with your right foot, straightening the knee, and move your entire torso slightly to the side.

Since the first movement caused the right punch to miss, the left straight lead is the next most often attempted strike (Fig. 89). Avoid this punch by shifting to the right. Note that since the left lead is normally not as controlled a punch, and considering the angle from which it must be launched, a more pronounced shift is required. It should be noted that since the target is the head, a movement of only a few centimeters may be needed to slip the punch. This level of skill comes only after many hours of practice, since the eye must visualize the trajectory of the incoming fist almost from its initiation. This sometimes makes the student susceptible to "fakes."

When throwing the left lead, the right hand normally falls to the right hip. This enables the enemy to continue his attack with a right hook to the head (Fig. 90). Remember that you have not as yet returned his attack or even touched him. Psychologically, he will think that a single punch may yet end the fight. He will also begin to lower his guard since he is not in the process of defending himself. Duck under the right hook as it arcs in from your left side.

From this point on, the drill is considered "classical" because the backfist (Fig. 91) is a characteristically Oriental technique and because the assailant may change his style of attack at this juncture. He has already thrown several unanswered punches and has not yet been "punished" for them (in boxing parlance, "make him miss, and make him pay," by counterpunching). Therefore, he may reevaluate his options. If he does not do so, he may attack with the backfist, as shown, or the left jab. Either or both of these attacks may be evaded by fading back away from the attack and arching the trunk. In a more combative situation, the hands would protect the body.

FIG. 87

FIG. 88

FIG. 89

FIG. 90

FIG. 91   FIG. 92

Having exposed his trunk area to you, your opponent will attempt a left hook to your liver, if he is a worthy boxer (Fig. 92). Avoid such a blow by employing the abdominal lift. Raise your arms in order to facilitate "sucking in the stomach" and to keep arms out of the line of attack. If this movement is performed and the elbows are pulled up and to the rear, the head juts forward, and the footing is lost.

In Fig. 93, the enemy continues his attack to the body with a right cross to the solar plexus. Twist to the left into a sitting horse stance on your left leg. Such a stance turns the entire torso out of the line of attack.

The enemy next attacks with a left cross to the solar plexus (Fig. 94). Again, employ the turning pivot to evade the attack.

In frustration, the enemy attempts the roundhouse right (Fig. 95), a common sucker-punch. Characteristically, this punch is brought up from the floor and may easily deteriorate into an overhand right. In either event, "bob," or

FIG. 93   FIG. 94

"sink," as the attack is launched (this movement is different from the "duck," which is a type of bending forward action). Relax both knees, and the center of gravity *(Hara)* is lowered vertically.

As the roundhouse right continues, weave under the punch (Fig. 96). Having lowered the center in the previous movement, push with your right foot. This action will prevent your body from dropping too low and causes the torso to shift to the left, causing you to weave under the intended attack. Note that the final position is the same as if the attack had been a straight right. If this one movement alone is mastered, the probability that the enemy will strike a blow to your head is reduced by half.

As seen in Fig. 97, the enemy tries a kicking attack. Assuming he is of a median level, he falls back over his platform leg and strikes out with a right crescent kick to your head. You must drop to one knee, thereby removing your head and torso from the upper and middle quadrants. This

FIG. 95

FIG. 96

FIG. 97

FIG. 98

technique is effective against the forward snap kick as well, but it leaves one vulnerable to the stomp-kick. As will be seen, the momentum of the crescent kick carries the enemy past your position.

The momentum of the crescent kick turns the enemy toward his right front corner, causing him to land with a cross-step-in-front stance (Fig. 98). At this point, you may elect to close with him and grapple, since his back is exposed.

The enemy continues to turn, dropping forward and executing a low leg sweep with his left leg (Fig. 99). If the range is such that only the lead leg is in danger, raise the lead leg out of the path of the sweep.

If the range to the enemy is such that both legs are in danger, employ the "hop" to avoid the attack (Fig. 100). Land lightly and easily on the other side of the enemy's leg sweep as it passes (Fig. 101). Before the enemy can regain his balance, spring over his lowered body (Fig. 102). At this point, execute the forward roll to break the fall as you land on the other side (Fig. 103). Continue the forward roll (Fig. 104).

FIG. 99

FIG. 100

FIG. 101

FIG. 102

FIG. 103

FIG. 104

As you begin to regain your balance, your opponent may turn in pursuit (Fig. 105), but you have by this time gained ten to fifteen feet of lead. It should be simple to avoid any further hostilities.

Ninety percent of enemy attacks can be successfully evaded once these movements have been mastered, even if strikes other than those illustrated are employed.

FIG. 105

6. ESCAPES AND REVERSALS

The entire thrust of the art of Ninjitsu is toward the concept of invisibility. The unarmed combat *(Kumi-Uchi)* system is divided into several components: 1) being unseen at the out-set, one's goal is to remain unseen for the duration; 2) being seen, one must vanish from view; and 3) being seen, cornered, or seized, one's goal is to escape. Having discussed the first two components of the art of Ninjitsu, we will now focus on the third.

Those involved in the Goju style of Karate tell the story of Master Yamaguchi. Yamaguchi, a prisoner of the Japanese, was thrown into a pit with a ferocious tiger. The karateka promptly kicked the tiger squarely on the nose, stunning it long enough for him to leap upon the beast's back and strangle it. The lesson to be learned from this story is that "when you are one with the tiger, he can find no place to tear with his claws or rend with his jaws." This tale is a good illustration of the underlying principle in most Kumi-Uchi techniques: get behind the enemy. In so doing, one becomes unseeable and virtually untouchable.

Techniques that may be used to avoid capture when one has been careless enough to give away one's presence within the enemy camp will be discussed here. We will begin with techniques in which the combatants are not yet touching, advance to those in which the enemy has secured a rudimen-tary hold, and examine several escapes or reversals.

It is imperative that you remember that all of these techniques are designed to ride the tiger. To make oneself invisible by moving to a position where the enemy cannot see you requires speed and daring, especially if your opponent has already launched an attack.

TURNING THE COLLAR PLATES

The technique of turning the collar plates was ancient when jujitsu was first systematized. The ancient samurai customarily wore their armor into battle, which considerably restricted their motion, especially compared to the unencumbered Ninja. It was soon discovered that one could seize the samurai armor by the collar (shoulder) plates which protected the warrior from the diagonal neck or shoulder cut, and literally turn his head to one side. Over the centuries, the technique has been modified, retaining its name since it so accurately describes the action.

The combatants may be facing one another, or they may have suddenly come face-to-face as the result of a pursuit or search (Fig. 106).

In any encounter, the fighter who strikes first has a half-second advantage over the fighter who waits for an opening. Therefore, to take advantage of a sudden face-to-face encounter, take a short step forward with your left foot and simultaneously strike your enemy on both shoulders with the double palm-heel strike. The opponent is thus pushed slightly off balance to his rear (Fig. 107).

As your opponent resists this backward push by leaning forward, use your momentum against him by turning his shoulders. This is an example of a *tenkan* movement, meaning that it takes advantage of the enemy's own movement rather than requiring movement on the part of the perpetrator. Following this movement, you can push with the left palm heel and simultaneously pull with your right palm heel to turn your enemy toward his right rear corner. If he is ar-

FIG. 106   FIG. 107

mored, grasp the aforementioned parts of the armor. If he is unarmored, this action will cause your opponent to be struck in the throat by your left forearm (Fig. 108).

Continue to turn your opponent by applying pressure to his shoulders while shifting your weight forward over your lead leg. Strike him between the shoulder blades with your right elbow. This blow will help keep him from adequately resisting the push, as well as driving some of the air out of his lungs (Fig. 109).

Using your left forearm, jerk his head back. Clamp your right hand down onto his left forearm in the classical Japanese strangle. Move your left foot to a point behind your opponent's left heel, and lean back slightly. This technique will prevent him from stepping away and help to "cross" his legs. (Note: Such crossing action slows the circulation in the affected limb, which will cause your opponent to pass out sooner from the strangle.) See Fig. 110.

FIG. 108

FIG. 109

FIG. 110

FIG. 111

From this position, you can drag your enemy out of sight as he passes out, or, as in the more ancient tradition, your fingertips are extended and the enemy's neck is dislocated by pulling back and down. This will work even if he is wearing full samurai armor.

This set of movements illustrates several important points about vanishing. First, it may not be necessary to flee or hide, but merely to make the enemy look away. Second, by making the enemy direct his attention to his own discomfort, his mind will not be concerned with much else. Third, while it is important that the enemy not see you, it is equally important that he not be allowed to signal that something is wrong.

TRICEPS PINCH

In the previous technique, we observed that the combatant who strikes first has the advantage. Barring the opportunity to use the shoulder-push-turn movements before the enemy can react effectively, and assuming that he is able to take his fighting stance, the Ninja have developed the following technique to again steal the initiative.

Assume a four-to-six posture with the lead hand held low. By leaning slightly away from the enemy, you may deceive him into thinking you are farther away from him than you really are. He will thus be drawn into range (Fig. 111).

Shift your weight forward over the lead leg and reach suddenly upward from below with your left hand. Strike the underside of your enemy's arm with the inside of your palm; immediately grip his triceps muscle between your thumb and fingers. Squeeze as hard as you can, directing the pressure against the inside of the upper arm with your thumb.

Try to locate the above-mentioned pressure point on the inside of your own arm. Halfway between the shoulder and elbow, under the biceps and above the triceps, lies a minute fossa (depression). Within this depression lies the brachial artery, as well as the primary branch of the brachial nerve plexus which controls the arm. By applying pressure at this site, and you will know immediately when you have found it, it is possible to numb the entire arm beyond the point of pressure. This element is critical, since it is clearly illustrated that one is vulnerable to the enemy's backfist at this point.

You need not fear that the enemy will pull away from this upper-arm grip, since your hand actually holds his humerus (long bone of the upper arm) rather securely. Any attempt to jerk free merely increases the pressure on the vital point of the arm, thereby inducing additional pain (Fig. 112).

At the moment that you pinch the triceps, your opponent will wince. Take this opportunity to lift his upper arm so that his arm is essentially over his own eyes. At that moment, vanish from his sight. The pain experienced in his arm should cause him to close his eyes reflexively (Fig. 113).

In order to execute the "lift," shift your weight over your lead leg and rise slightly from your previously lowered stance onto the ball of your left foot. At this point, the entire left side of the enemy is vulnerable to any attack you may wish to launch, but remember that the object is to disappear, not to merely gain the advantage in a fistfight.

Pivot on the ball of your left foot, and step quickly behind the enemy. Release your hold on his arms as you pass. Strike him firmly on the back of his shoulder with your right palm heel in order to drive him further to his left front corner away from you as you quickly duck out of sight (Fig. 114).

You could instead conduct a stranglehold now that you are behind the enemy, or you can execute a spinning back pivot over the ball of your right foot, which would place you behind your enemy's right shoulder.

From experience, it has been determined that the enemy will bend at the waist, bringing his arm to his chest. He will

FIG. 112

FIG. 113

FIG. 114

then grab hold of his biceps protectively. Two to three seconds will elapse before he sufficiently regains himself to even look for you. When he does look for you, he will turn to his left rear corner. You can then easily step into the Mi Lu Kata and remain invisible indefinitely behind him.

PALM-UP FINGER FAN

A third method by which the Ninja may gain the initiative before the enemy can strike presents itself as your enemy begins to raise his guard. From the four-to-six posture, prepare for the enemy to lift his lead hand defensively (Fig. 115).

Shifting your weight over your lead leg, swing your forearm, palm up and outward from the elbow, in order to cause the extended fingertips to rake across your adversary's eyes as the palm-up block passes over his shoulder. To use this action as a strike, you can extend the knuckle of your thumb and strike your adversary in the temple (Fig. 116).

As your opponent is forced to blink or turn away from the eye strike, turn your shoulders toward him. Cover your chest with your right hand. Rotate your left wrist so that your palm faces your opponent (Fig. 117).

Before your adversary can regain his vision, drive your palm-heel into his chin, forcing his head back and further obscuring his view (Fig. 118).

From this position, you have several possible avenues of action. You can rake down across your adversary's eyes with a left tiger-claw strike, or you can push back even further and throw your adversary backward. The Ninja could also vanish by quickly ducking out of sight to a place of concealment, or he can attack with his right hand. Another possible action is to strike the chin with enough force to cause whiplash action to the back of your enemy's neck, thereby knocking him out.

EYE FLICK

We have considered the means by which the initiative

FIG. 115

FIG. 116

FIG. 117

FIG. 118

may be seized from the enemy. Now let us consider a method of regaining the initiative should the enemy be the first to launch an attack.

The attack that is most commonly employed by adversaries who are unfamiliar with their opponent is the left jab. This strike seldom requires total commitment and does not throw the enemy off balance. Though it is an excellent probe, it can also be turned to a disadvantage by a skillful Ninja. Assume the basic fighting stance shown in Fig. 119 in preparation for the assault.

FIG. 119   FIG. 120

As the enemy shoots out his jab, block with an elbow-up block by rotating your elbow upward and turning your wrist back toward your body. By moving in to the jab slightly, the impact of the jab is forestalled, and the gap between you and the enemy is bridged. Note that this is accomplished by merely shifting weight over the lead leg (Fig. 120).

As the impact is felt and the jab is made to hesitate, immediately whip your forearm up and over your adversary's arm with your fingers extended. Rake across his eyes from the side with your fingertips. (A backfist might be used with the back knuckle directed against the temple.) This "slap to the eyes" must have the same action as a branch which has been pulled back and suddenly released. Once the strike is made, withdraw your forearm, making the motion of the eye-flick strike similar to the snapping of a whip. You may continue moving your arm in an arc, thereby helping to depress your enemy's lead hand (Fig. 121).

As your fingertips continue across your enemy's face and he is forced to flinch or at least turn his head, bend low from the waist, dropping out of sight. See Fig. 122.

Before the enemy can recover, cross-step in front by using the Heng Pu step. Pass the enemy on his left side, as

FIG. 121

FIG. 122

FIG. 123

FIG. 124

shown in Fig. 123. Alternately, one might pivot on the ball of the right foot and swing around to catch the enemy in a waist cinch from behind, or a back-out step can be used to move to the right side.

SLAP-DOWN EYE STRIKE

Next to the lead jab, the second most popular probing attack is the backfist. In the basic on-guard stances, prepare for an attack as shown in Fig. 124.

As the backfist is launched, deflect the blow with the

FIG. 125

FIG. 126

raised-arm block, a block not commonly taught in martial arts schools since it is primarily a setup for overhooking the arm prior to a throw. This type of block brings the side of the arm near the head, thereby placing a barrier between the fist and the intended target (Fig. 125).

As the strike is deflected and before the enemy can withdraw his arm, strike down onto his face with the extended fingertips of your left hand. It is not necessary to gouge or dig your fingernails into his eyes as you strike, since the slightest touch is usually sufficient to make the enemy blink. Note that in Fig. 126 the right hand is beneath the enemy's arm. From this point, it is possible to trap the opponent's arm or actually overhook the arm and break his elbow.

Pivot on the ball of your left foot and step behind the opponent with your right foot. As you do so, simultaneously strike his left shoulder with a right elbow strike, driving him forward and allowing time for you to escape from view (Fig. 127). Remember that he will not be able to see for a few moments due to the tearing of his eyes. We have thus again moved to a position behind the enemy, and the alternatives for action are as discussed previously.

FIG. 127   FIG. 128

ARM-DRAG TO STRANGLEHOLD

Just as it is possible for the enemy to seize the Ninja, it is possible to have the Ninja seize the enemy. In order to seize your opponent, it is essential that you move quickly from one movement to another. One must, however, know which technique is to be used before the initial contact is made in order to prevent the enemy from gaining the initial advantage.

Seize your opponent by his right wrist with your left hand (Fig. 128). Secure your grip as best you can, bearing in mind that if he is perspiring, the sweat on his arm will make it difficult for you to maintain a good hold.

Pull your opponent forward with your left hand, reaching for the inside of his arm. Catch his triceps with your right hand. Use the same pressure point employed in the triceps pinch to induce him to come forward as you shift somewhat to the side, simultaneously moving toward him. His balance will be broken forward by this ploy, but he will resist the pull. This instinctive reaction sets him up for the passing step (Fig. 129).

Quickly step forward with your right foot, bridging the

FIG. 129

FIG. 130

FIG. 131

FIG. 132

gap between the two of you. Release your grip on his wrist and slide your left forearm around the back of his neck (Fig. 130). Maintain the triceps pinch to prevent any counter-attack.

As he straightens in resistance to your forward pull, quickly execute a step behind him by pivoting on the ball of your right foot. Release the triceps pinch and whip your right hand behind his head. Grab your right biceps with your left hand. Allow your enemy's resistance to your original pull to push him into you as you clamp down with the stranglehold (Fig. 131).

FORWARD PIVOT

Should you be seized by the wrist, immediately pull against the grip as if you were trying to escape. This movement will cause your attacker to plant his feet into the ground and lean in the opposite direction (Fig. 132).

This predicament is particularly hazardous for the defender. Since the enemy has already shifted his weight in order to resist the pull, you should expect that he might either lash out with a roundhouse kick to your head or a side kick to your ribs. Since you are also being held prisoner by the wrist, you cannot evade either attack because you cannot move out of range.

Move to the limit of your arm extension, gaining as much distance as possible in preparation for your counterattack. You are now, unfortunately, also within range of the full extension of the enemy's attack as well. Since it is known that the end of the arc is the most powerful part of a technique, this situation is quite a dangerous one. Position your rear hand at the solar-plexus level, holding your elbow in near the ribs for protection. Since your weight is distributed in a back-stance position (70 percent on the right leg, 30 percent on the left leg), a leg sweep by the enemy could easily be avoided.

Before your opponent can attack, it is essential that you advance and smother his technique by being too close to him.

To reverse the enemy's wristlock, rotate your left hand (palm facing the enemy) in a counterclockwise circle. This will bring your wrist above and outside of his wrist. Break your wrist free by pulling against the little-finger side of his fist. The hold can thus be reversed, and you can seize his forearm above the wrist in an overhand grip. Shift your weight forward over your left leg and move in on the enemy. At this point, you may elect to break his elbow (hammer fist to the locked arm) or shoulder (shuto to shoulder joint) as seen in Fig. 133.

These two actions will deflect your opponent's arm across his centerline, negating any attack from that quarter. When the direction of the pull is reversed, the enemy's balance will be upset because he is leaning against that pull. He will seek to save himself by trying to shift his weight forward, thereby eliminating the danger of a lead leg attack. However, since his weight has now shifted forward, the probability that he will launch a spinning kick or backfist exists.

The application of the "pull-away/jump forward" type of reversal described here is characteristic of the jujitsu principle of balance *(kuzushi).* The more off balance your opponent becomes, the simpler it will be for you to control him. Utilize this pull-away/jump-forward tactic quickly and only as long as it takes to "set him up."

Pivot on the ball of your left foot, swinging your right leg half of an arc toward your right front corner. Whip your right arm around your victim's waist from behind while maintaining your grip on his left wrist with your left hand. Seize your left wrist with your right hand to secure the waist cinch (Fig. 134).

The forward pivot brings you behind the enemy; the arm-drag has brought him into position. Danger still exists in that he may execute a rear elbow strike or a heel kick to your groin, or he may reach through his legs and pick you up by your right leg. Even though you have reached a position of relative safety and secured a wristlock on your opponent by which he may be controlled, the technique is far from complete.

You can now shift your victim's left arm into a hammer-lock, hook his left ankle with your left ankle, and push forward into an ankle breakdown. Another option is for you to release your right arm and execute a lateral drop behind him for a heel-block takedown.

FIG. 133   FIG. 134

This is the most basic of the Hsing Tsia Movements, the forward 180-degree pivot (forward pivot).

REVERSE PIVOT

This technique works well against a fighter with a preference for the lead jab who is slow to recover and an attacker who prefers to seize the defender's right wrist with his left hand. In either event, rotate your right palm-heel in a counterclockwise manner with the edge of your hand toward your opponent. The arc is such that the right palm passes in front of the chest at throat level, intercepting the jab or reversing your enemy's grip. As a result, you can seize his wrist with an underhand grip. As these actions are performed, shift your weight forward over your left leg and twist toward your right front corner with your shoulders. Keep your left hand in front of your body defensively as you begin to push your opponent's fist across his centerline (Fig. 135).

If you employ this technique against the jab, let your enemy try to strike you at least twice while you are out of his range so that you can get a good sense of his timing. Also try to get him to slap his fist to one side. This will make your block faster and more accurate. At closer range, you can exe-

FIG. 135   FIG. 136

cute the Shotokan crossing forearm block. This block is achieved by wiping across the line of attack with your rear forearm, which is held vertically in front of your chest, and the impetus drawn from the twisting action of the shoulders and hips.

As you cross your opponent's centerline with his arm, he will be deflected slightly forward. Maintain your pressure against his wrist with the heel of your right palm to prevent any counterattack in which he would use his wrist (Fig. 136). You may elect to perform the one-hand elbow break at this juncture if you have gripped your opponent's wrist. Step forward and strike the back of his locked arm with your elbow as you pass. At the same time, quickly step forward and slightly behind his lead leg with your right foot. You are now behind him, outside the line of attack.

It is advisable to bump his shoulder with your own as you step in. This helps keep him off balance in the same direction, while some of his weight remains on his rear leg (helping to forestall any spinning-back technique he may employ in defense). In older times, it was also taught that one should swing the right leg, knee first, into the enemy's thigh or into the back of his knee to further disable him as you step forward.

Immediately after performing these actions, turn your head quickly to look over your left shoulder. (In dance, this movement is known as spotting.) You will thus be able to better keep your balance as you perform the back pivot. It is essential that you learn to spot in order to execute this technique or any other spinning-back variation; otherwise, such techniques will not be fast enough to be effective, and you will be off balance.

Cross-step backwards with your left leg while continuing to look over your left shoulder. Step as far back behind the enemy as possible. Pivot on the ball of your right foot one hundred eighty degrees to your left rear corner, and load your left sword hand near your right cheek as you spin behind the enemy. This technique must be completed in one smooth, flowing motion by the arc of the shoulders and the turning of the hips. Remember that the waist is the "banner" and must go into battle first. The spinning-back pivot momentarily places you back-to-back with the enemy. The momentum of the hips and shoulders, the maintenance of weight on the balls of both feet, and the pivoting motion over the right foot while shifting your weight to the left will carry you past your enemy. Try to stay as vertical as possible, since to do so aids in keeping your balance and allows you to pass closer (Fig. 137). As you clear your opponent's right side, whip out strongly with the left sword hand, striking him sharply on the medulla (base of the skull), seventh cervical vertebra (back of the neck), or side of the neck (if he is quick enough to turn into the pivot). Keep your right hand defensively near your solar plexus (Fig. 138).

If your object is to overcome the enemy, you have done so. If, however, your aim was merely to pass him, substitute a slap on the back of his head for the shuto, and step forward with your right foot a second one hundred eighty degrees. Repeat this technique. In this way, it is possible for you to pirouette out of range.

FIG. 137   FIG. 138

TURNING PIVOT

It is not always necessary to gain ground on the enemy in order to secure a position behind him. Any boxer knows the value of slipping punches and that the enemy will occasionally overextend himself, thereby exposing his back to attack. It is also possible to draw the enemy into the desired line of attack by feints or by pulling him to you.

The Japanese term *tenkan* means to pivot or turn aside. By utilizing the tenkan movement, one may go behind the enemy and pull him down directly against his line of balance.

In practice, assume a san-ti stance (70 percent/30 percent weight distribution over rear and lead leg, respectively). Allow your enemy to grasp your right wrist with his right hand. This action may be facilitated by stepping slightly to his outside line with your lead leg and extending your right hand into the field of fire. Keep your weight on the balls of both feet as you attain this position, as doing so will make it easier to shift your weight in the next movement (Fig. 139).

Bear in mind the principle of yielding and resisting the enemy's grasp. You want him to come forward, and you want to be behind him when he does so. As he seizes your wrist, immediately pull back strongly as if your attack were spoiled and you were about to retreat.

As soon as your opponent sets himself against you, reverse your pull and in a clockwise manner rotate your right hand with the palm up and facing your enemy. Release yourself from his hold. Continue to rotate your right palm until you can clamp down on your opponent's wrist with an overhand grip, thus reversing the hold and taking the initiative.

Since your opponent was pulling against you and suddenly there is no resistance, he will start to fall backward; the intensity of the struggle will determine how far he will be off balance. He will attempt to save himself by shifting his weight forward. As he does so, strongly pull him forward with your right arm. In so doing, you will induce him to topple toward his right front center. As you pull him forward, pivot on the balls of both feet, perpendicular to the line of attack. Shift your weight into a firm horse-riding stance. Reach over your opponent's arm with your left arm, and place your left palm, thumb-side against the throat, beneath his chin.

Lift his head by pulling back and upward on his chin while cupping it in your left hand. Block his right leg with your right knee so that he cannot step back and save himself. Maintain pressure against his arm at the elbow with your chest, and pull him over backward (Fig. 140).

ENTERING PIVOT

Employ this technique when you have to disarm an opponent who is holding a weapon in his right hand and launching a low hooking attack. In practice, however, the attacker begins by seizing the defender's left wrist with his right hand. He then seeks to pull the Ninja forward by this hold, while the Ninja in turn sets against the pull by lowering his center of gravity and assumes a modified horse-riding stance.

This resistance can be maintained only long enough for the enemy to commit himself to the pulling action, since the aim of this technique is to let the enemy retreat and to allow

FIG. 139   FIG. 140

you to pass directly in front of him with some degree of safety (Fig. 141).

This action might well be employed against an enemy who has a powerful grip against whom other escapes and reverses have failed. Logically, if one cannot free oneself from the grip, one should attack the next target of opportunity. In this case, that target is the elbow.

Note that in Fig. 141, the enemy's arm is bent as he exerts himself by pulling the Ninja toward the centerline. If you were to be in such a situation, your arm would be extended toward the enemy (but not locked straight) in an effort to stay out of range of his secondary attack.

As your enemy tries to pull you into his attack, cease to resist and move quickly toward him by executing a toe-out with your left foot, and step past his lead leg with your right foot. You will thus be outside the initial line of attack, but your back will be exposed to the enemy. As you begin this movement, swing your left arm as if trying to reach across your waist. Reverse that action and swing your arm, the elbow now bent, outside up and overhead as you step underneath. With your right hand, seize your attacker's wrist above the point where he has gripped you. As you step in, the added push of this arm, backed up by the momentum of the shoulders and hips, will aid in lifting your enemy's arm high enough for you to pass underneath. Bear in mind that you have not as yet escaped his grip, having only secured a counterhold in an effort to forestall a secondary attack from your attacker's left side.

In Aikido, the above-described technique is the first half of the entering *(irimi)* movement. In this instance, irimi means entering pivot. In seizing your enemy's wrist with your right hand, employ an overhand grip on the inside of the forearm. Catch your attacker's wrist in the web of the hand, between the thumb and index finger, and grip it strongly. Twist his arm, palm down, as you move in. This action will tend to bring your left wrist out of his hand by acting against the thumb side of the hold (Fig. 142).

Some martial arts schools advocate slapping the enemy on the left cheek as you swing his arm up in order to distract him. This slapping will also induce him to lean back (give way), thereby allowing you more room to pass him.

Pivot on the balls of both feet simultaneously, bringing your opponent's arm down past your left shoulder in a strong action, wrenching his shoulder and twisting his arm still further. His palm will now be facing upward and will be

FIG. 141

FIG. 142

slightly behind his back. If you have been unable to break his grip, bend the knuckle of your right thumb and place it against the tendons which run from the wrist to the hand on the inside of his forearm. Dig your knuckle into these tendons while maintaining pressure against the outside of his forearm with your fingers. These tendons control the fingers, and the applied pressure will force them to relax, facilitating your escape. When employing this method in order to force your enemy to drop his weapon, use the knuckles of both of your index fingers, since you can use both hands to hold his wrist.

You are now one hundred eighty degrees from your original position in a san-ti, or back stance. Jerk your left wrist toward your chest to free it from your enemy's grasp. You may elect either to place your left palm against his right elbow and exert downward pressure (causing his shoulder to dislocate), or you can use the jujitsu method of squatting into a horse stance and trap your victim's arm across the body. In either case, bearing down on his arm will make it possible for you to force your enemy to the ground (Fig. 143).

The goal, however, is to go behind one's enemy. To accomplish this, draw your left leg through the opening created by your passing, and step behind your opponent into a back stance. Your right leg should be in a forward position. You will now be further out of range of any counterattack.

Your right hand should maintain your grip on the enemy's wrist. Your left hand (now free) is brought into play by placing the thumb against the back of your opponent's hand and gripping the little finger side of his hand with your fingers. As soon as is feasible, shift your right hand to a similar position, with the right thumb lying alongside or across the left against the back of the hand. The enemy's wrist, now forced downward, is also forced toward the inside of his forearm (Fig. 144). This wristlock is known as *Kotegoshi*, and it

FIG. 143   FIG. 144

may be used to force the enemy facedown to the mat. By using the Kotegoshi, you can swing your enemy toward his right rear corner and into an obstruction (Figs. 144 to 146).

The elbow of your victim may be broken if you maintain the wristlock with your right hand and chop down onto his joint with a left shuto.

FIG. 145   FIG. 146

HEEL-BLOCK TAKEDOWN

Should your enemy quickly step forward and attempt to seize you with arms extended, swing both of your arms up and outward from the centerline, striking him on both biceps with a mirror block/shuto. Seize both of his arms by the muscle, pressing your thumb against the lower center of the muscle. Since nerves and blood vessels pass beneath the biceps, this grip will paralyze and numb the portion of the arm distal to the pressure point.

Having secured the hold, distribute your weight evenly over the balls of both feet to brace against the enemy's advance. Alternately push, pull, and push again to determine the state of his balance. Direct your actions against him at shoulder level, maintaining your own balance by lowering the center of gravity *(Hara)* slightly. Try to give the enemy the feeling that you are attempting to uproot him or push him straight back. It will be easy for him to resist this attack by bending forward at the waist, which is the movement you want him to make.

You must appear to be struggling with your opponent, keeping him just disoriented enough to prevent an attack. Hold his attention on the high line of attack, since this will set him up for your next movement (Fig. 147).

Once the desired state of imbalance has been reached, bend both knees. Quickly step forward and to your opponent's rear with your right foot, shifting into a forward-leaning stance *(zenkutsu dachi)*. In this stance, there is a 60/40 percent weight distribution over the lead and rear legs, respectively.

Push up on your opponent's left arm and drop your own left arm out from under his right (Fig. 148), striking him in the stomach with your left forearm as you pass beneath his left arm. Duck your head under and sweep past him in one smooth motion. Since he is braced against your push, he will

FIG. 147   FIG. 148

lean slightly into your attack. This will increase the effective-
ness of your forearm strike. The blow should be directed
against the point of the lowest rib on your opponent's right
side. This is the medical "alarm point" of Western medicine,
and it becomes tender when the liver is injured or diseased.
Boxers are familiar with this target, knowing that it is possible to render an opponent unconscious with a solid blow to
this area. The technique is known as the left hook to the liver
(Fig. 149).

Wrestlers will recognize the principle of feinting to the
head and dropping low to avoid an enemy's advance. This
technique, which has survived centuries of study and variation with little change, is simple, quick, and effective.

Having hooked your adversary's waist with your left arm,
execute a lateral drop-fall directly behind his back, landing
on your right hip. The momentum of swinging past your adversary and braking with your forearm will easily pull you
around to this position. The fall may be further facilitated
by pivoting on the ball of your right foot, which already lies
behind your enemy.

As you land, drive your right palm-heel directly upward,

FIG. 149   FIG. 150

striking your enemy's groin. This technique is sometimes known as the reverse-monkey stealing a peach, and it will totally incapacitate the strongest foe. In schools of the *Iron Hand ryu,* students are taught to seize the genitals and snap-tear them off. The practice method for this is initially to juggle small leather bags filled with lead shot, clawing each forcefully on each toss. In the later phases of training, iron balls are substituted for the sacks to develop the grip to a high degree (Fig. 150).

Alternately, those who study the sword-hand and needle-finger styles advocate a spear-hand strike to the groin or a needle-finger attack to the target known as the Vessel of Conception No. 1. This acupuncture point lies directly in the center of the scrotum and is the point of origin for the thrusting channel of Chinese medicine. Even a light blow to this site will cause severe injury to the genitourinary tract.

Complete the technique by wrapping your right arm around your enemy's right thigh from the inside and seizing his belt in the center of his back if possible (Fig. 151). Roll to your left, pulling your opponent over backward by blocking both of his heels with your body. As he topples, use your left hand to guide him over you. This is actually a very gentle technique in terms of disrupting the opponent's balance.

If your opponent is familiar with the art of falling *(ukemi),* he may escape by executing a back roll. If, however, he is unfamiliar with the principles of meeting tatami, he will almost certainly try to save himself all the way down. In so doing, he will land mostly on his shoulders and the back of his head (Fig. 152). The only danger in this technique is that the enemy will realize your intent and sit quickly downward on top of you. Two methods exist for preventing this from happening: the first is to use the upward groin strike previously mentioned, and the second is to utilize the fluidity of the motion. Bear in mind the principle of riding the tiger. He cannot bite or claw you as long as you remain on his back. Getting there and staying there are always somewhat risky (Fig. 153).

REAR BEAR HUG ESCAPE NO. 1

Ninjitsu, the Art of Invisibility, may be considered pragmatically as the art of sneaking up on the enemy from behind. Needless to say, this should *never* happen to the Ninja. If your assailant succeeds in gaining a position behind you and seizes you in a bear hug, the quickest and the simplest escape is as follows:

Drive the back of your head into your assailant's face. You need not strike with all your force, since even a moderate blow of this type should break his nose. When striking with the rear head butt, try to avoid hitting his teeth, since you may possibly cut your scalp in the process (Fig. 154).

Bend sharply at the waist, striking your enemy's abdomen with your buttocks in order to break his hold (movement not shown). Reach between your legs to seize his leg behind his heel (Fig. 155).

Stand erect once more, lifting your enemy's leg off the ground by pulling forward on his ankle and simultaneously

FIG. 151

FIG. 152

FIG. 153

FIG. 154   FIG. 155

bracing against his thigh with your hips. As he lands with a solid backfall, grasp his ankle with your other hand to secure the grip, and sit down on his knee. Be extremely careful when practicing this movement so as not to injure your partner. Approximately forty pounds of pressure is required to break the knee in this manner (Fig. 156).

REAR BEAR HUG ESCAPE NO. 2

If your enemy is clever enough not to place his head in a position which will permit you to use the rear head-butt, assume that he has secured his hold (Fig. 157). The following movement can also be used as an alternative to the previous movement.

Shift your weight to your right leg and cross-step with your left. By doing so, you will have sufficient space in which to strike the enemy in his solar plexus with an elbow stroke.

FIG. 156

As this is a sensitive area of the body, even a moderate blow will be effective; you should, however, strike as many times as needed to secure your release. The aim is to get one hand free, and the easiest way to do so is to break the bear hug (Fig. 158).

As his grip is broken, immediately strike downward with your hammer-fist, striking your adversary on the pubic symphysis. Sufficient force may break the pelvic girdle, effectively crippling him (Fig. 159).

As your adversary bends forward from the hammer-fist strike, whip upward with your backfist, striking him in the face. A moderate blow to the face—the nose in particular—will cause tearing of the eyes and stun your victim (Fig. 160).

Pivot on the balls of both feet and overhook your adversary's head with your right arm, pulling him forward and down. At this point, swing your right leg upward in preparation for a backfall (Fig. 161).

Drop straight downward, pulling your enemy down with you (Fig. 162) until the top of his head is driven into the ground (Fig. 163). Push his body to one side (Fig. 164).

FIG. 157

FIG. 158

FIG. 159

FIG. 160

FIG. 161

FIG. 162

FIG. 163

FIG. 164

REAR BEAR HUG ESCAPE NO. 3

Since different adversaries apply a rear bear hug in various ways, and what works against one enemy may not work against another, here is another technique you may utilize to escape from such a hold.

Try to lift your arms upward against the grip of your opponent's hold. Such an action will cause him to set himself against your movement. Shift your weight to the right (Fig. 165).

Seize the little fingers of your opponent's hand and pull them either backward toward his wrist or outward away from his other fingers. Continue to pull his fingers until he releases his grip. At the same time, drive the heel of your left foot downward onto his instep, thereby breaking the bones in his foot (the purpose of making him set was to enable you to break these bones).

When the martial arts were first taught in the West, the heel-stamp was part of every self-defense course. It has fallen into some disrepute over the years because it is thought by many to be ineffective. If properly performed, however, this blow will crush the long, thin tarsal bones of the foot, not the toes! Such an injury will prevent any adversary from pursuing you (Fig. 166).

Having broken your enemy's hold you have forced him to widen his stance in an effort to avoid the heel-stamp. Sit straight down and slightly extend your left leg (Fig. 167).

Roll backward between your enemy's legs, and grab both of his ankles from behind to prevent him from stepping away. Execute a front snap-kick to his solar plexus with your left leg (Fig. 168).

Roll backward with your hips, and hook your enemy's left knee from behind with your left ankle. Maintain your grip on his ankles. As your hips lift off the ground, reach out with your right foot and hook your opponent's head, which

FIG. 165

FIG. 166

FIG. 167

FIG. 168

is now lowered due to the solar-plexus strike. Pull him forward, using the strength of your legs. Bear in mind that he cannot step away because of your double ankle-block (Fig. 169). One might suspect that the enemy need only fall backward or sit down to block this throw. Such is not the case, for should he even attempt to do so, you need only release either of his ankles and strike him in the groin with the appropriate palm-heel. The impact of this attack and the remaining ankle block will cause him to execute a twisting fall over his trapped ankle.

As your opponent falls forward, withdraw your right leg from beneath him and allow him to take the full impact of the break-down fall on his head and chest (Fig. 170). If necessary, you may scramble forward while maintaining the leg grapevine on his left leg, and strangle him into submission.

FIG. 169   FIG. 170

FRONT BELT THROW

In deference to Judo, this technique might better be labeled "sash-pull-down." In the classic *Obi-nage,* one hand seizes the opponent's belt while the other seizes the back of his head. The receiver is alternately pushed and pulled over by the thrower's weight and is pulled onto his back. In contrast, the Ninja belt throw is more of a battlefield technique. Like the collar-plate turning technique, the belt throw evolved from a need for simple, effective, close-in takedowns.

Assume your enemy has secured a front chokehold (in this case with his forearm). In order to free yourself from this hold, place your right hand, palm up, under his left elbow. Your left hand should lie in the crook of his right elbow (Fig. 171).

Alternately pull down with your left hand and push up with your right palm, turning your head toward the left. The pressure against your windpipe will thereby lessen, enabling you to break the chokehold. Simultaneously, shift your weight over your right leg (Fig. 172).

As you slip out of the choke, drop to your right knee and seize the enemy's belt with your left hand. His balance will have been broken to his left rear corner, the exact position you now occupy (Fig. 173).

With your left hand, strongly pull downward as the enemy leans toward his left in an attempt to regain his balance. Draw your left knee toward you so that he is driven onto your impaling knee as he falls forward (Fig. 174). Push his body away from you by drawing your left heel behind you.

Do not be afraid to be beneath the enemy's body, since his body may protect you from unintended incidental blows during a melee.

FIG. 171

FIG. 172

FIG. 173

FIG. 174

7. POSTSCRIPT

To influence the lives of men, one must remain outside the circle of forces which affect them.

Thus says the Sage, the Man of Knowledge, the Sensei whom we all follow. The Ninja should remain detached from those who would employ him, as well as from those whom he would freely serve. One may conclude from this advice that the Ninja are rather "cold," emotionally speaking. And they are, at least insofar as they do not allow their lives to become entwined with the fortunes of those not on the Path to greater Knowledge. Nor are they involved in causes themselves, for they would then be as lost as those who seek transitory goals such as gold, power, and so on.

Remember that the Ninja still exist today; in fact, they flourish in the Kabuki theatre. Ninja are the stage handlers, swathed in black, who set the scene and affect the lives of men (the players), but they are not characters in the play themselves. In this way, they are one with nature, for while onstage, they represent Nature, and Nature is eternal and everbalanced.

So it must be in the life of the Ninja then . . . to play in the Great Game, yet be untouched by it; to remain honed to fighting edge, prepared, capable; to act in preservation of the balance Nature intends or for the pleasure of acting; to strive always to become a Man of Knowledge and lead by example, being both feared and loved. In this way one may pass his time in relative peace and harmony.